KARATE

The Complete Course

GUINNESS

KARATE
The Complete Course

A step-by-step guide from first move to first competition

TOMMY MORRIS 6TH DAN BLACK BELT

Edited by David Mitchell
Designed and produced by
The Bowerdean Press Ltd
London SW11

© The Bowerdean Press Ltd and
Guinness Publishing Ltd 1987

Published in Great Britain by
Guinness Publishing Ltd
33 London Road, Enfield, Middlesex
Reprinted 1990

British Library Cataloguing in Publication Data
Morris, Tommy
    Karate: the complete course
    1. Karate
    1. Title
    996 8 153   GV1114.3

    ISBN 0 85112 836 X

All rights reserved. No part of this publication may be reproduced, stored in a retrieval system, or transmitted in any form or by any means, electronic, mechanical, photocopying, recording or otherwise, without prior permission in writing of the publisher.

Typeset in Great Britain by
Dorchester Typesetting Group Ltd, Dorchester, Dorset
Printed and bound in Great Britain by
Southampton Book Company, Regents Park, Southampton

**'Guinness' is a registered trade mark of Guinness
Superlatives Ltd.**

The Martial Arts are potentially dangerous: the author, producers and publishers will accept no liability for damage or injuries resulting from the performance of techniques described in this book.

The cover pictures and all pictures in the book were taken by Mike O'Neill of Mike O'Neill Associates.

CONTENTS

FOREWORD

Tommy Morris is a well known karateka of many years international standing. He was a well known competitor before becoming an international referee and is now the Chairman of both the European Karate Union and the World Union of Karatedo Organisations Referee Committees.

He is respected for his fairness, impartiality and knowledge of karate competition and I am delighted to endorse this book as a valuable contribution to international karate training.

Jacques Delcourt,
President, European Karate Union
President, World Union of Karatedo
Organisations

Tommy Morris is both an international competitor of note and a world-class referee.

HISTORY OF KARATE

The Japanese fighting art of *karate* comes from a self defence system used by the natives of Okinawa. Okinawa is a large island to the south west of Japan and during the fifteenth century its king prohibited the carrying of weapons, so an interest in unarmed combat consequently developed.

Karate was first called *to-te* but this was later changed to *kara-te*, meaning 'China hand' in recognition of the large contribution made to it by Chinese kung fu. When the system was introduced to Japan, the name *kara-te* was kept but the meaning was changed to 'empty hand' as a device to help its promotion.

'Empty hand' didn't just mean having no weapon, it also meant empty of all evil desires and intentions.

There were several schools of Okinawan karate, each differing slightly from the other in some aspect. These differences were introduced to Japan and gave rise to the four major schools of karate which are:

> The Goju Kai
> The Shito Kai
> The Shotokan
> The Wado Kai

There are other schools but they are generally regarded as offshoots of these four styles.

From Japan, karate spread into America and Europe and it has developed to the point where it is now recognized as a world sport by the International Olympic Committee. The controlling body for world karate is the World Union of Karatedo Organisations and in Europe, the continental organisation is known as the European Karate Union.

Karate is not just a sport. It also contains elements such as discipline, respect and philosophy which go beyond sport. It is also a very effective system of self defence.

Competition Karate

Competition karate is a safe and exciting combat sport. Techniques are controlled so they don't land hard and the rate of injury is quite low. One of the most worrying aspects of any combat sport is the possibility of brain damage through hard blows landing on the head.

The rules of karate competition are particularly tough in this respect and any competitor hitting another with insufficient control gets either penalised or disqualified.

Not all karate competition is of a combat sport nature.

EARLY COMPETITION

I actually organised the first international match in Britain when I invited the French Team to Scotland in February 1966. This came about through my association with Henri Plee of the Academie Française d'Arts Martiaux in Paris.

Each bout lasted a full five minutes compared with the two or three minutes of today's bouts. There was little if any face contact and for that matter, few scores! I remember that in my bout against Jean-Pierre Lavorato, we pounded each other for the full five minutes and spent no small amount of time pursuing each other off the area and almost into the audience. Yet despite the number of techniques exchanged, I was the only one to score. No-one seemed to know very much about how the bout should be judged!

It seemed that to score a full point, you had to actually drop the opponent! A very hard impact to his body that merely made him stagger only merited a half point and in another bout against the French fighter Dominique Valera, he kicked me so hard in the ribs that the next day I was walking about as though crippled. Yet he got only a half point for it!

The first British match with France took place in March 1966 and it was followed in May by the first European Championships in both of which I fought as a member of the British team.

Because there was such a shortage of officials, we used one referee and a mirror judge. We didn't know it then but this was later to become the accepted method of judging.

Shobu ippon or 'one point' competition was the first widely accepted form of sparring competition and the first competitor to score with a perfect technique won the bout. This concept of the 'one shot' bout has remained with karate to the present day and is why an unlimited number of scores is not accepted.

The idea was to hit the opponent with a technically correct technique which if it hadn't been controlled would have caused serious injury. After delivering this fearsome blow, it was equally important to pull the fist or foot back quickly and keep attention focused on the opponent in what the Japanese call *zanshin*.

After a while one point competition became very boring to watch because the fighters did nothing but circle each other warily the whole time. Since a single mistake usually signalled the end of the bout, contestants stuck closely to the easiest and least dangerous techniques such as reverse punch.

The one point bout was scored by a referee, an arbitrator and four judges who sat in chairs on each corner of the mat. They signalled their opinion by waving red and white flags and blowing whistles!

A *shobu sanbon* or 'three point bout' was introduced a little later but at first it wasn't a true three pointer because as soon as one contestant got a clear two point majority, he won the bout. After a year or so, the system again changed to a true three point bout.

Early competition tended to be boring.

EARLY COMPETITION

It is a problem devising tactics when you don't know which technique scores and which does not.

The mirror referee system was again used in the 1977 Paris Junior Championships because only thirteen officials turned up. However it worked so well that it was accepted soon after as the norm for all future three point bouts.

No-one ever quite knew (and many still apparently don't know to this day!) what a permitted level of face contact was, so for a while, none at all was allowed. This caused contestants to stop protecting their faces and changed the nature of competition away from realism. As a result it was decided to allow the lightest touch.

The problem is that the degree of face contact is subjective in that one referee may consider it light whilst another thinks it too heavy.

The idea of *mubobi* was then introduced with the object of making competition still more realistic. Mubobi required you to take proper precautions to safeguard yourself from injury when attacking but unfortunately the first translations were inaccurate and it came across as 'wasting time'! It was not until later that the correct meaning became apparent though it remains little used in modern karate competition.

Another misunderstanding arose over the interpretation of *jogai* or exit from the area. At first it was thought to mean escape, in which case the referee had to assess whether the move was intentional or not. It was only during the Akron Technical Congress that the true meaning – that of simply exit – emerged.

The coach played a large role in early matches. He could protest the decisions of the refereeing panel whilst the bout was in progress and as you might imagine, this led to interminable wrangling. In the end, things got so bad that a rule was passed making it impossible for the coach to protest except against actual errors in rule application. Even then the protest had to be submitted in writing.

Nowadays the coach is not even allowed in the competition area and as a result, bouts are more enjoyable and are interrupted far less often.

It is my opinion that the present rules of competition have developed as far as they can. There may be improvements in detail still to come but basically they are the best we've ever worked to but we still have to make the rules more understandable to the wider audience by means of such things as clearer scoring displays.

Perhaps obvious discussion between the referee panel could be eliminated by using small personal radio communicators. Two stationary judges seated on raised platforms would have a very clear purview of the match and be able to give their opinions on a score quickly by this means. Also of course they would leave the competition area clear of people who otherwise keep getting in the way of the television camera.

We shall see!

THE RULES OF COMPETITION

The first stage in winning a karate competition is to look the part of a winner.

Let's begin by looking at the rules under which you will compete.

First of all the competition takes place on a matted square so that if you fall or are swept your landing is cushioned. Karate competition must never take place on hard floors because of the risk of head injury arising through a chance trip or fall.

The square in which you compete is eight metres by eight metres and the edge is clearly marked by tape or mats of a different colour. There is a second indicator inside the boundary which serves to warn you when you are approaching the edge of the area.

Turn up for the competition in a clean white karate suit (called a *karategi*). Make sure it is neat and not ripped or covered with loud badges. Don't roll your sleeves up because they can form hard cutting edges if you do. Wear a pair of clean white fist mitts with no more than one centimetre of hard foam padding over the knuckles. Your thumb must be free of padding so it can fold in properly when you make a fist, otherwise it can sprain.

By all means wear soft shinpads. These are very useful in preventing bruising.

In some competitions you will be allowed to wear a combined shin and instep protector, so check with the organiser or your club coach to see what the rules for that competition say.

A groin protector is useful for male competitors but make sure it allows full hip movement yet doesn't float around. Do not wear the cups that slip into a jockstrap.

Although not compulsory – do wear a gumshield. Not only do these protect your mouth and teeth, they can also reduce concussion caused by a hard face blow. But you do need to have them properly fitted to get maximum protection.

Girls should also wear a chest protector in the form of a sports bra, or a custom-made plastic shield worn inside the karategi jacket. Don't use a pin to fasten the jacket across your chest – wear a clean white teeshirt underneath instead.

If you can't see to compete without your spectacles, then either get a pair of soft contact lenses or give up the idea of karate competition. Do realise that wearing contact lenses during competition is your decision and if they contribute to injury or you lose them, don't blame the referee!

Don't wear earrings during competition because they may get yanked out or bashed into your mastoid bone. Necklaces will get broken and/or cut your neck, whilst rings can mark the opponent. If you can't get your rings off, wind surgical tape around them.

If you are a Sikh or a practising Rasta, check with the organisers early on to see if you can wear your headgear. Don't expect too much cooperation though if you just turn up on the day and demand to wear it.

Karate competition is all about respect – respect for the opponent and respect for yourself. Therefore do turn up looking scrubbed and well groomed, with short clean nails and neat hair.

Your bout will be controlled by a referee and a mirror referee – the latter is sometimes

THE RULES OF COMPETITION

A full point is awarded for a perfect technique such as this roundhouse kick *(left)*.
The kick must be carefully controlled to avoid injury *(below)*.

called a judge. The bout will run for two minutes if you are a female or a male contestant under twenty one years old. It will last three minutes if you are a male above twenty-one.

The end of the bout is signalled by a bell or buzzer operated by the timekeeper. To let you know when time is running out, the timekeeper will give a shorter ring when thirty seconds remain. When the bout is stopped for any reason, the clock too is halted. All scores and penalties given during the bout are written down by the scorekeeper.

To make sure everything proceeds as it should, an arbitrator sits just off the area and watches each bout.

To win your bout you must score up to a maximum of three full points, either as such or as a combination of half points and/or full points together. It is impossible to score more than this during any one bout.

A full point is awarded for a perfect technique, whereas a half point is given where the technique is slightly imperfect. To get your full point, use a strong technique and apply it powerfully but with absolute control to a scoring area of your opponent's body. Time it carefully so it catches the opponent just right and pull it back afterwards.

That's all you have to do!

If your technique wasn't perfect but it did catch the opponent off-guard – such as a blow into the back – then you may still get a full point. Perhaps you tried a difficult combination technique such as a footsweep and punch, or a roundhouse kick to the head

and it wasn't quite perfect. In those cases, the referee may well recognise your effort and give a full point.

If your opponent commits a foul or can't continue through no fault of yours, then you will be given the victory and three full points.

When you go for a score, aim at the opponent's face and head (but watch your control!), or go for the chest, stomach and back. You won't get a score for attacking the groin, though you will receive a warning or penalty.

Keep in the area when you try to score because if so much as the tip of your heel is outside, you won't get that point. On the other hand, if you are driving your opponent out of the area with your forceful attack and score just as his heel goes out of the area and before the referee spots it, you can still score.

THE RULES OF COMPETITION

Superiority of technique can prove decisive in an otherwise tied match.

Don't expect to score if you attack the opponent after the referee has stopped the bout. You won't score either if you attack after the end of bout signal has gone – even though the referee may not have stopped the bout promptly. The time-up signal means no more chances to score!

When two people successfully attack each other at exactly the same time, neither score is given. The key word here is 'successfully' because it may be that one attack actually missed but the other didn't. In that case, only one attack was actually successful and scores though both happened at the same time.

When the bout is over, the referee compares the scores and if you got more than your opponent – you win! If there was no score, or if you and your opponent scored equally on each other, then the referee checks with the judge to see if there is agreement on awarding a win through superiority. This means that one of you used more skilful techniques, or always seemed to have the upper hand.

If a verdict can't be reached through this method, then the bout is given as a draw.

In a team match, a draw is no problem but in individual bouts, there has to be a winner through to the next round. So it will be necessary to fight a two or three minute extension to the bout. This extension is called an *encho sen* or 'sudden death' and the first to score takes the victory.

When two teams draw on the number of individual bout wins, the referee adds up the points each team scored in all of its individual bouts and the team with more points wins. If

Whichever technique you use, you must be capable of controlling it.

the teams remain neck and neck, then a deciding bout is fought between one contestant chosen from each team. If this too ties, a sudden death extension is fought and a decision reached.

You are allowed only the lightest possible touch when you attack the face – any more and you are penalised. If you use a high kick, your control must be no less careful.

You are not even allowed to touch the throat! Of course, if your opponent trips over the mat and impales himself on your fist, then it's hardly your fault and the referee will take the trip into account and probably not disqualify you.

Trained karateka are quite strong in the body, and techniques which land with a sharp impact tend to be the rule, rather than the exception. However, if you succeed in actually damaging your opponent with a body attack – look out!

Look out too if you appear to deliberately kick your opponent in the arm, shin, ankle or knee. Whilst a foot sweep is actually aimed at the ankle (i.e. not the shin or knee joint) it is a recognisable and permitted technique used specifically to unbalance your opponent. A stamping kick into the ankle will not be regarded as a valid foot sweep and you will be penalised for using it.

Use techniques which you know you can control. It is very difficult to bring a descending axe-kick to a total and sudden stop but there are some people who can do it. On the other hand, there are those who are unable to control even a simple reverse punch and are forever injuring the opponent.

Do ensure that you operate an effective guard whilst you are attacking.

For failing to control the impact of your technique, so it was just slightly too hard, you will get a warning at the very least. Don't depend on getting a warning though. You can lose the bout immediately on the basis of a single instance of contact!

If impact was harder but still not too serious, then you will immediately pick up a penalty which loses you either half a point or as much as one point.

Depending on what you got the first time, another slightly over-the-top impact in the same bout will definitely earn you a penalty. You will either have a half point or full point awarded against you. Do it yet again and you could lose the bout.

As I said a little earlier, don't go over the edge of the competition area because if you repeatedly do so, you will be penalised. The penalties work the same way as that described above. The first time you step out, you will get a warning but the second time results in a penalty costing you a half point. The third time you step out incurs a penalty of one point and one more time out loses you the bout.

Another quick way to earn penalties is by blazing into the attack with your chin stuck out in front. The referee will expect you always to take proper care of your own safety, so make sure you keep an effective guard. Even when you deliver a good score, don't drop your guard and dance about waving your fist because this will ensure you don't get the score but do get a penalty!

Do remember that if you get a penalty in the bout for whatever reason and then have to fight an extension, that penalty is carried over into the extension and one more slip no matter how slight, will cost you the bout.

Since we are talking about karate competition and not about wrestling, don't try to grab your opponent unless it's to put in a fast scoring technique. Pushing and shoving is not good karate and you will get warned for doing it.

Only your best behaviour is good enough in karate competition. Act in any other way and you may find yourself not only getting disqualified from the bout but banned from the tournament altogether! Even your mates can get you into serious trouble too if they behave in such a way as to bring disgrace on karate whilst you are competing.

Bear in mind that karate is a combat sport and if you receive a chance hard blow, don't reel around looking agonised! The doctor will see if you are injured and the referee will be able to judge the force of the blow without you trying to underline it.

Woe betide you if you pretend you received an injury and didn't!

If you do get a hard bang in the head, you may well be withdrawn from the competition and its no use your complaining because it's your health at stake. When the doctor diagnoses head injury, it means no more sparring for at least four weeks.

Begin your career in competition by learning these rules. If you don't know them, how can you compete with confidence? Karate competition still uses a lot of Japanese expressions and so I have listed these and their meaning in the glossary.

THE IMPORTANCE OF ETIQUETTE

It is said that karate training begins and ends with courtesy. This is one of the things which sets karate practice aside from many other disciplines, except that in modern competition it seems to be going by the board. This disturbs me very greatly because without etiquette, karate competition will lose its unique character and become something else like table tennis or five-a-side football.

I would like to think that karate competition is more than a game because with the level of control required, there must be a degree of trust between opponents. Karate competition is *not* the same as self defence. It is *not* the same as real fighting but the concepts are there all the same. Therefore the rules must be followed if people are to compete with reasonable safety.

If I know the opponent is really going to hit me, then I'm not just going to stand there, bow and wait for the referee's commands! It is no longer a game then.

You must be capable of strict self-discipline and be prepared to listen to and accept the ruling of the referee. All the shouting and bawling in the world isn't going to move the referee in your favour, though it may result in you getting penalised!

Although you may feel the referee's decision is incorrect, most often it will be you that is in the wrong. But if you feel you do have a legitimate complaint, then accept the decision

and then have your protest made through the correct channels.

Remember that the referee is human too. If you walk onto the area and bow politely, then fight fairly and within the rules, you will receive a fair and proper judgement. If you walk on aggressively, skimp on the bow and fight with a bad attitude, the referee may incline away from you — whether intentionally or not. The referee panel must after all be able to concentrate upon the technique and not be distracted by animosity or bad attitude and so the sensible contestant will ensure a fair assessment by behaving correctly.

I have seen a number of contestants with exceptional ability who have simply destroyed themselves by their bad attitude. They became so big-headed, so full of themselves, that they lost sight of what they were trying to do.

Certainly you must always fight to win but remain within the rules both in practice and spirit. Keep your temper. If you can't manage to do that, then karate competition is not for you!

We actually practise *karate-do*, the 'way' of karate and within this discipline, we try to conquer our own ego. If we abandon the 'way' and give way to a continuing loss of etiquette, then our competition will lose its character and become just another sport.

Use all means at your disposal within the rules to win. Don't be a good loser.

ARE YOU THE RIGHT SIZE AND SHAPE?

There is little doubt in my mind that physical considerations such as size and shape can play a major role in your performance at elite level. If you want to be a world champion, begin by selecting the correct parents! This applies in other sports too and if you are built to be a marathon runner, then you will never make it as a world champion powerlifter and vice versa.

The larger skilled karateka has a distinct advantage over the smaller but equally skilled opponent. Smaller fighters move more quickly but in a team situation, they can face real physical danger because a heavier and larger opponent's idea of control may be damaging to the lighter person.

The ideal team karate competitor is tall, has long legs and arms and is fast, flexible and agile. If you have a smaller build or lighter weight then compete in your weight division of individual events – it's far safer anyway!

Size on its own is not enough. The big, lumbering person is at a disadvantage in WUKO competition because the lighter and faster adversary can exploit slow responses.

Taller people have longer muscles which allow them to make greater usage of flexibility for long range accurate kicking techniques. The best international competition kickers are invariably lean individuals with long legs.

Shorter and stockier contestants may have explosive power and speed but they often have trouble with flexibility and find it more difficult to use kicks effectively.

Top karateka are fast, flexible and agile. On average men are more powerful than women.

Fat is inert tissue – it is like carrying a weight around with you. Do get rid of surplus fat by increasing the amount of physical work you do. A strict diet is often counterproductive and it is better to modify your eating habits rather than take on a fad diet that you have no possibility of maintaining throughout your competitive career. The next chapter contains more information about nutrition.

Although women are said to have faster reactions than men, a male fighter of perhaps under 60 kilos will almost always defeat a similarly sized and qualified female. Because the female carries a higher percentage of body fat, then weight for weight she will be less muscled than her male counterpart. Certainly upper body power is lower in females than males but I'm sure that isn't the only reason.

The gender gap may well have something to do with it in that boys are encouraged to fight and play combative games whilst girls are persuaded to play with dollies. This means that a lad will have already used his fists in the playground by the time he joins the karate club. The girl, on the other hand, may never have closed her fists and fought before her first karate lesson.

Within obvious limits, age is not the barrier that many people think it is. It may take longer to reach the same standard as younger students but with sensible training, you can still achieve a surprisingly high performance.

PRACTICAL NUTRITION

There is growing evidence that people who exercise regularly, eat properly balanced diets, don't smoke and avoid stress, live longer and are less likely to suffer from heart-disease, strokes or cancer.

It makes sense to follow a healthy life style, but it is absolutely essential, if you are ever to realise your full potential. There is a popular saying, that you are what you eat. It follows therefore, that there is no place in the athlete's diet, for the regular consumption of junk foods, with its high content of saturated fats, sodium and chemical additives. Be careful in the amounts of red meat you consume too. Even with all the visible fat trimmed off, lean steak still has a very high fat content. More important, it may also be contaminated with the chemicals used to promote high meat yield. Go easy on eggs, although they are very high in assimilable protein, they also contain a great deal of cholesterol, a substance which has been linked with heart disease.

People in the West generally consume too much fat and protein and not enough carbohydrate in the form of whole grains and cereals.

To delve deeply into nutrition is beyond the scope of this book, but to achieve a balanced diet you should try to consume foods from the five main groups every day.
(1) Milk group: skimmed or semi-skimmed milk, yoghourt, cottage cheese, lower fat cheeses such as Gouda, Edam, etc.
(2) Meats: poultry, fish, beef, eggs, etc.
(3) Vegetables: fruits, vegetables, legumes, nuts, etc.
(4) Grains: breads, cereals, pasta, etc.
(5) Fats: vegetable oils, butter, margarine, etc.

Roughly 65% of your diet should come from grains, fruits and vegetables and the remaining 35% from milk and meat groups.

Remember, as an athlete you need carbohydrates for energy and you should try to get your energy needs from the complex carbohydrate foods, already mentioned. These will supply the energy levels required, along with the roughage and fibre your body needs. Getting your energy in the form of chocolate and sweets is not recommended, as these simple carbohydrates can enter the bloodstream with a rush and about an hour and a half after consumption, your blood

Fat is inert tissue and offers little benefit to the karateka.

PRACTICAL NUTRITION

Maximum performance requires good nutrition.

Sensible vitamin supplements can do no harm and may be beneficial.

sugar and energy level drops well below what it was before. Bear in mind also that refined sugar contains nothing but energy and is devoid of nutrients, and what you don't use, the body stores as fat.

I haven't seen many fat world karate champions lately.

Proteins form the basis of the body's muscle maintenance and repair mechanism, but don't think you'll get big muscles from eating big steaks since the body's ability to assimilate protein at any one time is limited. Of the meat group, fish is most easily assimilated by the body, followed by poultry.

Fats also supply the body with energy though usually only during prolonged aerobic activity. They are however one of the most abundant sources of vitamins A, D, E and K.

What about vitamin supplementation? Well the answer you get depends on the source you approach. Ask the supplier or manufacturer and he'll make an impressive case for taking supplements. Non-vested interest sources on the other hand will tell you that there is no case for taking extra vitamins.

Theoretically speaking, if you do take a nutritionally sound and balanced diet, then you should be getting all the nutrients you need. In the real world however, much of today's food is processed and stored for fairly long periods and much of the vitamin content may be lost before it gets to you. There does appear to be some evidence, that slight vitamin deficiencies do occur, and I personally take a multi-vitamin and mineral supplement occasionally.

Don't go overboard though; keep the doses at reasonable levels, since you can take too much, particularly the fat soluble vitamins such as Vitamin A.

You might think you are doing very well, living on pizzas and burgers and smoking 60 cigarettes a day, but all I can say is you'll do very much better if you take my advice.

As the WUKO Chief Referee I know all the World Champions of the last decade. None of them smoke, though a couple of bronze medallists do.

GETTING FIT

Pick those techniques you are likely to use a lot in competition and work hard at them.

A karate bout lasts only two or three minutes but during that time, you will be moving in bursts of maximum speed involving both limb speed and whole body movement. Your kicks must easily reach to the opponent's head and you must be agile enough to position yourself in the best place to score at any instant. You must be able to work out what your opponent intends by means of cues taken from his behaviour pattern and respond with the correct move at an early stage.

All this requires a certain mix of physical fitness factors, the first of which is the aerobic component.

Aerobic fitness is the ability of the lungs to take in and absorb oxygen from the air, and the effectiveness of the heart and blood vessels in transporting that oxygen to the working muscles. This is the first fitness system to improve because it is the platform that all the other components of fitness rest upon. Aerobic fitness is gained from low intensity extended duration exercises such as jogging, swimming and cycling.

The object of aerobic training is to get your heart rate into what is called the aerobic training band and keep it there for 15-20 minutes. The aerobic band lies between 70-85% of the maximum heart rate for a person of your age.

To find your aerobic training band simply deduct your age from 220 and then multiply by 70% and 85% and you have the lower and upper training limits

e.g. For a 20 year old $220 - 20 = 200$
$$200 \times 70\% = 140$$
$$200 \times 85\% = 170$$

The lower limit is 140 beats per minute and the upper limit is 170 beats per minute.

There are other more accurate formulae but this one is good enough for general use. If you are very unfit you would be better advised to limit your heart rate from 60% to 75% of maximum for the first two months or so.

However, do not set yourself an extended programme of aerobic training; you want to be fit for karate, not jogging.

Anaerobic fitness is the ability of the muscles to work longer in the absence of sufficient oxygen. It is built upon short duration high intensity work. No karateka can keep going flat out for even three minutes because the muscles reduce in efficiency as the amount of lactic acid waste material builds up.

Therefore the purpose of anaerobic training is to condition your muscles to tolerate and function well in spite of high levels of lactic acid.

One of the most interesting ways to train anaerobically is by performing a long and arduous kata several times over at full combat speed. Not only does this achieve an anaerobic training effect but it is also useful for opening up neural pathways to facilitate skill acquisition.

If you do a large number of kicks one after the other, before long your legs get tired. You are not out of puff though because all the tiredness is localised in the working muscles. Your training must therefore take in what is called 'local muscular endurance'.

Select the techniques you are likely to use a lot in competition, then work hard and continuously at them. The more training of this nature you do the longer you will be able to kick and punch before slowing down.

Muscular endurance can be increased by body weight exercises or weight training, but be careful as too much endurance training may lead to a reduction in speed.

Strength is the ability of a muscle or group of muscles to work against resistance. Power is the muscle's ability to work *quickly* against resistance. Power is more important to the competing karateka than brute strength. Power can be enhanced by using weights.

Speed is the ability to quickly move a limb and/or whole body in response to a situation, and agility is being able to suddenly switch direction without fumbling or getting caught on the wrong foot. Both can be improved by using special training drills.

Flexibility refers to the range of movement of a joint and so far as karateka are concerned, the hipjoint is the one that commonly needs most flexibility training. The range of movement there can be increased by stretching the muscles which hold the joint together but at the same time, those muscles must not be weakened otherwise your joints become unstable.

Flexibility training involves stretching exercises and is best done after a good warm-up session.

PREPARING TO COMPETE

You can't train for an important competition on a one hour per week training schedule because skill acquisition and fitness training require more than that. You will need to train three times a week for fifteen to thirty minutes just for aerobic fitness at the lowest level.

Ultimately the amount of time you spend training will depend upon how good you want to get. Being the best competitor in your club will not require the same commitment as being a top national all-styles performer. You alone must decide on your level of commitment but this will of course be revised as your interest in karate grows and your skill increases.

You may have joined karate for other reasons than doing well in competition and then discovered a natural aptitude for it – one you never knew you had. This can cause you to switch tracks and reappraise your practice.

Your coach is extremely important in ensuring your correct preparation. The good coach will make sure training sessions are interesting and varied and unless you have a strong character it becomes all too easy to skimp on training. The good coach will help by imposing a training schedule and insisting that you regularly meet targets such as gradings.

Left to yourself, you may be content to remain at your present skill level and decide to miss gradings. This leads to an abandonment of the overload principle of training and without the need to peak for an event, incentive is lost. You are merely marking time and not improving.

Being a top level competitor in any sport, particularly in karate, requires a large commitment of time and energy. How far do YOU want to go?

If you cannot generate enthusiasm to press on, then sooner or later you will give up karate training in favour of some other pastime.

A training record is vital for karateka and coach alike. I for example, keep a record of every one of my students and this allows me to pick up quickly on absences.

During the early stages, it is vital to train regularly or you will miss a great deal of fundamental training that is not repeated later. Gaps in training may well explain why a particular student is not able to perform certain techniques.

If this fails to explain it then I will look at how the student performs to try and see why they are having difficulty. There may be a physical or mental reason for the problem.

For example, when a karateka has difficulty with the roundhouse kick, I have found that it is generally due to two factors. The first is a lack of knowledge of how the body is coordinated during the technique. Perhaps the beginner has missed the fact that the supporting foot is supposed to rotate and he tries to swing the hip around whilst keeping the supporting foot pointing straight ahead.

The second is an overall lack of hip flexibility. If the latter, I give the karateka a flexibility test to confirm my opinion and if I am right, I introduce a remedial flexibility programme to the training.

If all else fails, then we must look for an alternative technique and go around the blockage. Having bypassed it, we can then return at some later point. The important thing is not to let failure in one technique affect the whole of training.

Measure your performance improvement against a properly kept training record.

THE FIRST THREE MONTHS

To get you ready for successful competition I have divided your training programme into three periods. Each contains both fitness training and skill acquisition. I have arbitrarily given each a span of twelve weeks, assuming three or more sessions per week.

In this, the first three months of training, I am assuming that you are not very fit but know a little about karate.

Begin your training session with an aerobic fitness programme. If you have access to an equipped gymnasium, use a cycling or rowing machine and a power jogger. This kind of equipment housed in a warm and well-lit facility is excellent on freezing cold or wet, dark days. The power jogger has a cushioned treadmill so spine and knees do not get the same hammering they get from a pavement or road.

If you don't have access to this kind of equipment then try swimming, cycling, or cross country running. People who aren't good swimmers may not find swimming to their liking and end up getting muscle fatigue rather than an aerobic training effect. If you don't live near a grassed area then cycling may be better for you than jogging.

Keepfit classes are not just for women. Both the stretching and aerobic training involved will benefit all novice karateka.

Whichever system you select, you must get your heart rate up into the aerobic training band. If you are unfit, then aim for the lower reaches of the band and gradually increase training pace as your fitness level improves.

Go directly from aerobic training to local muscular endurance exercises such as press-ups, sit-ups and squats. Press-ups work the upper body muscles. To get the best training effect, do each one correctly. Position your hands more than shoulder width apart and support yourself on the palms of your hands and the balls of your feet. Keep your body in one straight line and don't let it sag, *fig. 1*.

Lower yourself until your chest brushes the floor, *fig. 2*, and hold there for an instant before sharply pressing yourself back to an arms straight position. Don't bounce up and down because it lessens the training effect.

1

2

There are a number of variants of this exercise, which train the involved muscles in a slightly different manner. Turn your hands inward so the fingertips brush each other, *fig. 3*, then drop down until your elbows all but touch the floor, *fig. 4*. Pause for an instant to avoid a bouncing effect and then drive yourself back up. Another variant places your two fists close to each other in the midline of your body, *fig. 5*. As before, lower yourself onto your fists, pause, *fig. 6*, and then drive back up again. *Caution: closed fist press-ups are not recommended on a hard flopr.* A good triceps trainer uses two study chairs spaced so your bottom can fit between them. Stretch your legs out in front and sit back down between the two seats, supporting body weight with your arms. Lower yourself slowly between the seats by bending your elbows and when you reach bottom, drive yourself back up again. As with the press-ups – don't bounce down!

3

4

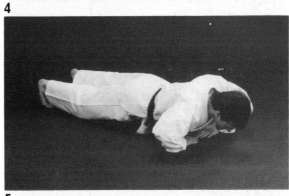

5

6

7

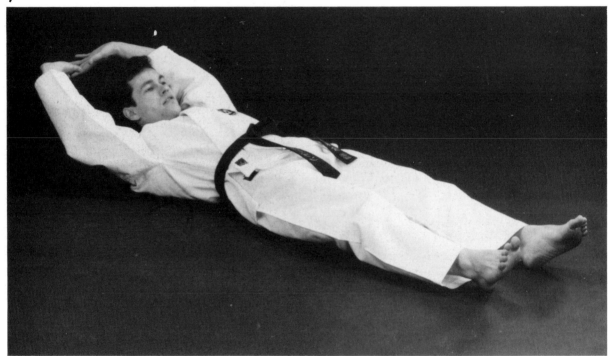

There are several ways of doing sit-ups. The way not to do them is to straighten your legs and bounce up and down, *figs 7 & 8*. Even worse are straight-leg raises. *Don't do them.* I advise that all sit-ups should be performed with bent knees, *fig. 9*. This position then allows the pelvis to tilt back, disengaging the *Iliopsoas* (a large hip flexor muscle) and eliminating possible damaging strain to your lower-back. Remember that the main job of that large sheath of muscle that runs from your rib cage to your pelvis, apart from holding your gut in, is to pull your chest towards your lower abdomen; it has nothing to do with bending at the hip joint.

8

This is why so many people performing sit-ups, develop strong hip flexors and never see much improvement in their abdominal muscles!

10

Remember that you are trying to isolate the abdominal muscles, so there is no need to raise your lower back from the floor. When you do you are using other muscle groups to complete the movement, *fig. 10.*

9

THE FIRST THREE MONTHS

If you cannot do sit-ups without your feet lifting from the floor, hook your feet under something solid, or link legs with a partner, *figs 11 & 12*, though be aware that this method reduces the exercise effect on the abdominals.

Do another exercise whilst your legs are linked with a partner's. Keep your shoulders off the floor and punch with right and left arms alternately, *figs 13 & 14*.

11
12

13

14

THE FIRST THREE MONTHS

My favourite abdominal muscle trainer for the person who can manage normal sit-ups is the 'abdominal crunch'. To do this, bring your heels close to your buttocks and either put your hands behind your head, or fold them across your chest. Lower your chin onto your chest and try to lift your back up and off the floor, so your chest approaches your pelvis, *fig. 15*. Don't pull on the back of your head!

Hold the full-on position for a few seconds and feel the contraction in your abdominal muscles as they hold your shoulders off the floor. By bending your knees and not anchoring your feet you prevent the powerful hip flexors from assisting and therefore throw a greater work-load on the abdominals.

Either do a series of repetitions of crunches to get the best training effect, or alternatively hold the full-on position for five or ten seconds and repeat it as many times as you can.

Try a swivelling sit-up by twisting your body as you raise it off the ground and pulling your knee back to touch the opposite elbow, *fig. 16*. Lie back and come up again, this time touching the other elbow to knee, *fig. 17*.

I also recommend reverse abdominal crunches in which you bring the knees up and then try and raise the hips off the ground. Hold the full-on position for a short time, then lower the hips and partially extend the legs.

15

16

17

18

Complement the training effect of abdominal exercises with hyperextensions. Lie on your face and clasp your hands behind your back or behind the head. Arch your back and point your toes so your shoulders clear the floor, *fig. 18*. If it will help, have a colleague hold your feet down. Do not raise your chest too far off the floor, *fig. 19*, and only do a few of these.

19

20

Free squats are excellent leg muscle trainers and you should aim to do between 25 and 100, depending upon your level of fitness. Stand with feet about shoulder width apart and turned slightly outwards, *fig. 20*. Slowly lower into a half squat until your thighs are parallel to the floor, *fig. 21*, and the knees pointing outwards above the toes. Drive up quickly to an upright position.

Do not go down into a full squat especially if you suffer with knee trouble. Do not bounce down into the squat because this can overload the knee joint.

21

To try kick-squats, bend the knees (back straight), *fig. 22*. Thrust back up quickly, performing a high front kick as you do so. Kick on each leg alternately, *figs 23 & 24*. Keep your arms to your sides and close the hands into fists. 30/50 of these is normally enough for the average karateka.

22

23

24

THE FIRST THREE MONTHS

When you are thoroughly warmed up as a result of the above training, tackle the flexibility programme. As a beginner, you will be generally stiff and the first three months' of training will reflect this.

Starting from the top, turn your head to one side, *fig. 25*, pause, then turn it in the other direction, *fig. 26*. Lean your head back as far as you can, *fig. 27*, and then bring it down onto your chest, *fig. 28*. Lean it to one side, then to the other. Finally roll your head around your shoulders, first one way, *fig. 29*, then the other, *fig. 30*.

Lift and rotate your elbows so your shoulder blades move around. Straighten your arm and put the palm of your hand against a wall, then rotate your body so the chest is stretched. Reach over and upwards behind your back and try to link fingers, *fig. 31*. Extend your arms out from the shoulders and twist your body as far as it will go in one direction, then in the other.

25

26

27

28

29

30

31

Lie on your back and bring your elbows up so your hands rest either side of your head. Push up with your feet and hands so your body rises off the floor and arches, *fig. 32*. Hold this position and then let yourself return to the resting position. Repeat this several times. Beware! Don't do this exercise if you have had any trouble with your lower back.

32

Stretch the hamstrings by leaning over and down, touching the floor in front of your feet. Your knees point straight ahead and your feet must be slightly parted. Straighten up and lean back as far as you can, so combining a hyperextension with the stretch. As a variant of this stretch, bend your knees so you can put the palms of your hands flat on the floor, *fig. 33*. Whilst keeping your palms flat, straighten your knees, *fig. 34*. Do not bounce.

33

34

Another way to stretch the hamstrings takes place when you lie on your back on the floor and keeping one leg extended, bring the other as close to your chest as possible, *fig. 35*.

35

Go into a long forward stance, with back leg straight and your heel pressed firmly to the floor. Arch your back and drop your rear hip towards the floor so as to stretch the *Iliopsoas* muscle, *fig. 36*. This muscle group can be injured when you lower your centre of gravity to stop punch the opponent, so stretching is important.

36

Extend your forward stance still further whilst keeping your body upright and finally step out further still, dropping your rear knee to the floor, *fig. 37*.

37

THE FIRST THREE MONTHS

Sit down and extend your legs in front of you, keeping the backs of your knees pressed firmly to the floor. Lean forwards and hold the position of greatest stretch for at least ten seconds, *fig. 38*. Repeat this a number of times before opening your legs as wide as they will go, *fig. 39*. Take hold of your heels or if you prefer, lean forwards with arms in front, *fig. 40*.

Hold the lowest position for a minimum count of ten seconds then switch to a side-to-side movement, holding your head down on each knee alternately, *figs 41 & 42*.

40

42

THE FIRST THREE MONTHS

43

44

Slide the feet up and press your soles together, *fig. 43*. Put your elbows inside your thighs and lever your legs out and down so the knees approach the floor, *fig. 44*. Hold the lowest position.

Extend one leg out in front of you and cross the other over it. Take hold of the ankle and rotate your foot first one way, then the other, *fig. 45*.

45

Support yourself against a wall and bring your foot up and back so you can grab the ankle. Draw the leg upwards and towards the small of your back, *fig. 46*. Changing position slightly, bend your knee as far as possible and take hold of your foot, pulling it up tight against your bottom, *fig. 47*. Get your breath back and simultaneously stretch the quadriceps muscle by sitting in a formal kneeling position with feet flat under you. Keep your back absolutely straight and sit right back on your heels, *fig. 48*.

48

49

50

Press the palms of your hands together and push your forearms downwards, *fig. 49*. Then put the backs of your hands together and push upwards, *fig. 50*.

After this work out, you are ready to begin skill training.

Begin by taking a good fighting stance with knees bent equally and a 50/50 weight distribution, *fig. 51*. The front foot turns in about 45° degrees and the rear turns slightly more. The rear foot is not in line with the front but is offset three or four inches to one side to provide a firmer balance, *fig. 52*.

51

52

The front guarding arm is open and extended forward from the body. The elbow is bent and the forearm brought into the midline of the body, tips of fingers in line with the top of the shoulder. Keep your hand open and you will find it easier to move more quickly, *fig. 53*. The other arm is closed into a light fist in front of the chest.

Keep your front guard well out from the body and it will keep the opponent at a safer distance. Bringing your forward guard in close will encourage the opponent to approach that little bit closer, forcing you to keep moving back to maintain safe range.

Another advantage of keeping the guard well forward is that it then requires only a small movement to deflect attacks close to their origin when they have not yet picked up full power.

53

Do not stand with the feet too much in line or stance stability is adversely affected, *fig. 54*. A stance that is too short, *fig. 55*, will not withstand a strong attack and is more susceptible to attacks such as sweeps. When you are at a goodly distance by all means take a high stance but when distance is closed, settle into a lower and more stable stance.

If you face your opponent directly, he will have a very large area to attack. Therefore stand at an angle and immediately the available target area is diminished, and incoming techniques that aren't exactly targeted tend to glance off to either side.

When you stand square on, your deflection of an incoming attack has to be very effective or it is simply redirected slightly to the side. If on the other hand you stand at an angle, only a small deflection will knock the attacking technique clear of any target.

54

55

56

57

58

To do a reverse punch, drive off the rear leg whilst sliding forwards on the front foot to get range absolutely right, *figs 56 & 57*. Twist your hips until they turn forwards-facing, *fig. 58*, allowing your chest and back to arch so tension builds up in the spine. The reason for this will be explained later on.

Drive your fist forward, *fig. 59*, and at the same time pull back the leading guard hand so it finishes near the side of your face, *figs 60, 61 & 62*. Aim to strike your opponent solidly and high in the body, withdrawing the punching fist quickly to emphasize a score.

Practise this punch in both advancing and retreating modes so you can use it for attack and defence. As your opponent moves towards you, step back with the rear leg and draw back the front to maintain correct range.

Use body movement to make a fine range adjustment but don't telegraph your intentions. Your punch is most effective when it is not expected, so unless your opponent is concentrating totally upon his attack to the exclusion of all else, your reverse punch is likely to be seen at an early stage.

Therefore disguise it with a block that knocks the opponent's guard to one side, or alternatively first feint with a front snap punch.

59

60

61

62

THE FIRST THREE MONTHS

Fast competition back fist uses less body movement than is required if you want to develop maximum actual power with it. Start from a normal fighting stance, *fig. 63* by raising your striking arm until the elbow points at your opponent's head, *figs 64 & 65*.

Move your rear fist away from the chest and extend it forwards. As you do this, slide forward on your front leg to get fine range adjustment. Don't trail your rear foot too far behind and if necessary slide it up a little to maintain stance length.

As you finish moving, let fly with the back fist whilst rapidly pulling back the opposite arm, *figs 66 & 67*. Withdraw the striking arm quickly after the score is made.

63

64　65

66　67

Bring body weight forwards behind the strike but don't lead with your chin! The strike must look potentially powerful and be delivered from a stable stance to stand a good chance of scoring, *fig. 68*. Jumping back fist combinations tend not to be scored by knowledgeable referees.

68

THE FIRST THREE MONTHS

Try reverse back fist too! This is similar to the regular form except that you strike with the opposite arm to the leading leg. To get the same range, twist your hip more fully and concentrate more weight on the front leg, *figs 69, 70, 71, 72 & 73*. As before, pull your strike back quickly and re-establish a stable fighting stance with the minimum of delay.

69

70

71

72

73

Back fist strike is a good response to a mid-section reverse punch and you can use either type in conjunction with a low deflection block, *fig. 74*.

74

75

76

77

Competition front kick must involve as little telegraphing as possible so pick your kicking knee up as quickly as you can, *figs 75 & 76*, swinging it up and forward to cover your lower abdomen, *figs 77 & 78*. Drive both hips forward as the lower leg moves quickly up and into the target with heel low and toes relaxed, *figs 79 & 80*. Your foot actually travels from floor to target at an angle of around 45°. Keep your weight back as you kick or you will be more susceptible to scooping block.

Drive off the floor by thrusting down with the ball of the foot and lift the knee quickly. Try to avoid tensing the leg and acceleration will be higher. Keep the knee up and maintain an elbows-in unchanging guard so the chance of an effective counter-punch is lessened.

Stretch a karate belt between two chairs to train at getting your kicking leg high enough. Lift your foot up and over it as you kick.

78

79

80

To have the best chance of success, the foot has to travel in the most direct way to the target and this is particularly important with roundhouse kick. Some schools of karate require you to lift your foot to the side of your body before swivelling it across and into the target, *fig. 81*. This telegraphs your intent and is too slow for WUKO competition.

81

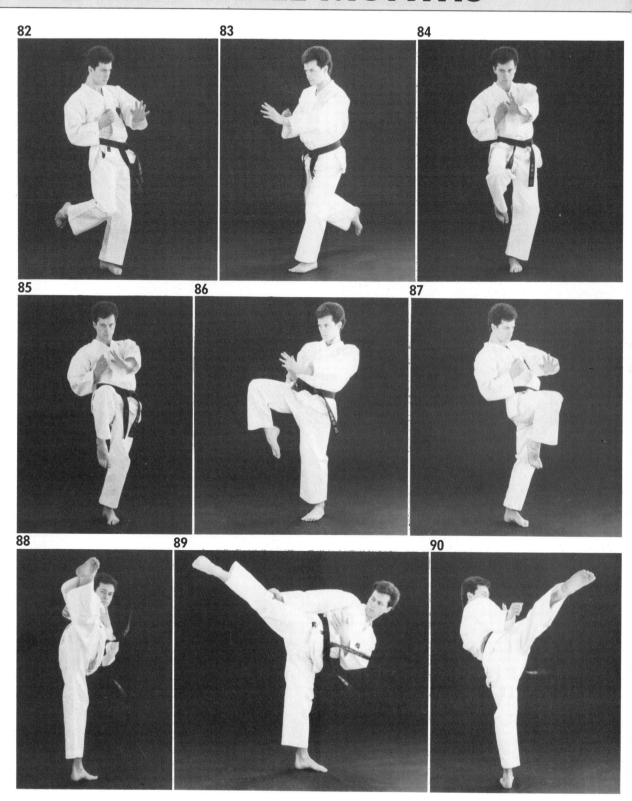

A competition roundhouse kick starts off like a front kick, with the foot thrusting hard off the floor, *figs 82, 83 & 84*. The knee rises quickly to kicking height as the body leans away from possible counter-attack, *figs 85, 86 & 87*. Though your opponent may be aware that you intend kicking, it will not be clear at this point which kick you intend to use.

The supporting leg continues to swivel powerfully so the kick describes a rising diagonal arc into the target, *figs 88, 89 & 90*. To get the correct angle of delivery, the supporting foot must rotate through at least 90°.

Strike the target with the instep, turning your toes down to avoid injury.

91

92

Reverse roundhouse kick also starts from the now familiar knee raised and guarded position, *figs 91 & 92*. Swivel on your supporting leg and lean back so the foot rises in a reverse arc, the sole impacting on the target area, *figs 93 & 94*. Point your toes to avoid landing with the heel, which could severely injure your opponent.

Reverse roundhouse rarely scores unless it is used against the head so always practise it at that height.

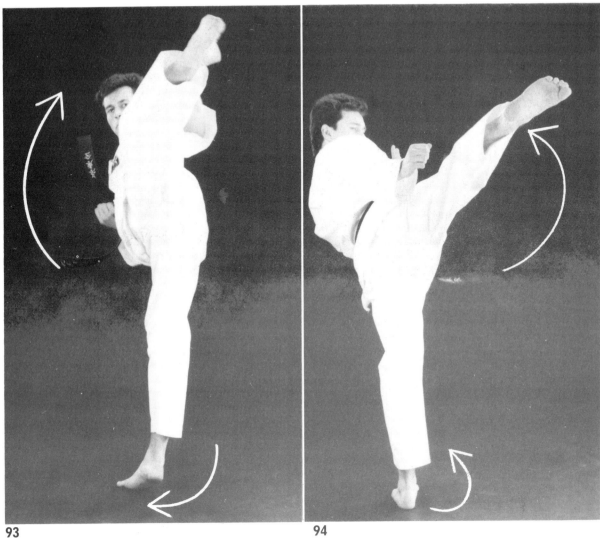

93   94

95

96

Slapping block is a fast counter to divert an incoming punch to the face or body. Carry your forward guarding hand well out from the body and as the opponent punches, slap across into his punch with the palm of your hand. Immediately the block makes contact, step in and throw a solid mid-section reverse punch.

Don't overblock! It is sufficient just to knock an attack slightly to the side. If you overdo it, you may commit too much to what turns out to be a feint, exposing yourself to the follow-up technique.

Scooping block takes an incoming kick and deflects it to one side by striking it with the hand, *fig. 95*. Use your palm, the back of your hand, or make a fist and block with the thumb side of the forearm. Do not scoop up from underneath the kick and do not block close to your own body.

The object is to cause maximum deflection of your opponent's kick, *fig. 96*, so you have ample opportunity to follow up with a scoring technique, *fig. 97*.

Block from a strong stance with the forward knee forcing outwards. If you need to adjust range, take a short slide back on the rear foot but it is unlikely you will have enough time to sidestep and twist the hips fully.

These then are the basic techniques to be practised during the first three months of practice. Work at them many times over until you can perform them quickly, accurately and with good control. In other words, acquire sufficient skill to do the techniques correctly.

A mirror will help because it shows what you are actually doing rather than what you think you might be doing. If the coach tells you to move your hip more during a particular technique you will be able to see that you are doing the necessary. Mirror training can be done at your own pace and allows you to cover the topics you feel you need to.

A final word of caution at this point. When you try these techniques against the air be careful not to damage the joints of your body – especially those of the elbows and knees. To reduce the chance of injury don't fully straighten your arms and legs during hard basic practice – even though it is traditional to do so. Halt movement by muscle action and don't rely on the joint itself stopping your technique.

GETTING YOUR SCORES SEEN

Many techniques are used in karate but in karate competition, only a small number provides the bulk of scores awarded. This includes:

1. Reverse punch (*gyakuzuki*), *fig. 98*.
2. Roundhouse kick to the head (*mawashigeri jodan*), *fig. 99*.
3. Back fist (*uraken*), *fig. 100*.
4. Reverse roundhouse kick to the head (*ura-mawashigeri jodan*).
5. The front kick (*maegeri*), *fig. 101*.

In addition to these, the sweep and stamping kick is now a common full point scoring combination whereas previously a punch was used to deliver the score itself. Whatever technique you do use, remember that in karate competition, speed and accuracy count far more than effectiveness.

98

99

101

100

GETTING YOUR SCORES SEEN

In general terms punching techniques leave the user less open to counter than do foot techniques and so are probably safer. High kicks do leave you in a very vulnerable position compared to a technique where both feet are firmly planted on the floor. Moreover your attacking leg is in the way of a fast follow-up during a high roundhouse kick, and it must be pulled back before you can even think of countering. A punch by comparison can always rely on immediate use of the other fist if required.

Novice karateka often use the wrong technique from the wrong distance and in the wrong manner. For instance, the most efficient use of roundhouse kick requires the opponent to be out of punching range and moving into the kick. If the opponent is moving backwards or in the opposite direction to the kick its effect will be lessened and it may not score.

The punch works well when the opponent is actually making an attack. Move inside it and counter to the body. The punch also works well when you have broken your opponent's balance or distracted him with a feint. Make sure that the punch you use looks powerful if you want to maximise your chances of scoring with it.

Fast snap punches off the front fist, *fig. 102*, often don't score because the referee doesn't feel there was enough power behind them. Other times they don't score because they move so quickly and over such a short distance that they are quite simply not seen for long enough for the referee to decide whether they scored or not. On the other hand, there is no mistaking the solid thump as the same punch contacts the opponent's chest.

So from a competitive point of view aim your punches at the body, though this is not of course to say that you shouldn't use a fast snap punch to the face as a feint.

GETTING YOUR SCORES SEEN

103

Be careful when using plain reverse punch as an attack because the opponent may see it coming and both deflect and counter-attack, *fig. 103*. I make a habit of thrusting my punching arm forwards before I move my body because it will get my punch into the target before telltale body movement provides an unmistakable cue. I would not however do this in a real fight because it robs the technique of too much power.

Two additional tips are to keep your face impassive so as not to betray intent, and launch yourself in a straight line at your opponent.

Although back fist has generally less potential power than a well executed snap punch it is nevertheless more easily seen and scored because of its longer action. Moreover using the elbow means that the technique is more precisely controlled and the fact that it is normally applied to the side of the head gives it more lee-way.

Roundhouse kick is used for best effect at near maximum range. Don't use the shorter range variants which impact with the ball of foot because this configuration involves tensing muscles in the front of the lower leg, slowing the kick right down.

Lean away from the kick to take your body out of line of counter attacks. Stand with your supporting leg in line with your opponent's leading foot, *fig. 104*, and this will help reduce the chances of a counter.

Many karateka mistakenly believe that you must kiai to attract the referee's attention but this is nonsense.

Kiai is not just a loud shout, it is a means of concentrating energy and this can be done by simply pursing the lips and breathing out in a short staccato gasp. If you try to push a car to get it moving, shouting won't help! If as you heave, you make a sharp exhalation in the form of a grunt, you will be making a proper concentration of force through kiai. Many old masters of karate will tell you to close your mouth when you kiai to prevent dispersing the force.

This is actually what the experienced referee is looking for. A loud shout often signifies the absence of power in the technique.

104

THREE TO SIX MONTHS

Maintain your earlier training schedule and in addition take on some extra work. Let's begin by looking at an alternative form of aerobic exercising using weights. Use this to increase your aerobic capability and push your heart rate towards the top of the training band by selecting weights which are about 40% of what you can manage to lift for one repetition. Set up a circuit of different exercises such as the following:

Sit-ups; overhead presses; biceps curls; triceps push-downs; bench presses; straight leg dead lifts; squats; leg lifts.

Do 20-30 repetitions of each exercise before moving to the next. Go from squats to sit-ups, from bench presses to leg lifts, etc. Check that your heart rate is well into the aerobic training band by gently pressing two fingers into the side of your neck near the windpipe. Count for 6 seconds only. This is not an accurate measurement but it will suffice. If, for example your age is 20 and your pulse rate is less than 14 beats per 6 seconds, then you must work harder at the circuit. If above 17, slow your pace down because there is little aerobic benefit from going above the training band, and in some cases it may actually be dangerous to work your heart too hard.

The object is to complete the circuit within a set period of time, perhaps 15-20 minutes. Go for a faster circuit as you get fitter and increase the number of repetitions. As fitness continues to build try doing the circuit twice. Take rests only as dictated by your heart rate, keeping it in the upper portion of the training band throughout.

Now is also the time to begin building local muscular endurance using harder exercises. Move the weights quickly during a number of repetitions rather than by shifting a very heavy weight slowly. Between 20/40 repetitions are needed for endurance training and the training weight to be used depends entirely upon you.

106

107

Strengthen weak muscle groups by doing between 5/10 repetitions of the following exercises with heavier weights:

squats
military presses
chins
bent over rowing
biceps curls
triceps extensions
straight & bent leg dead lifts
cleans

Do bear in mind that you are not bodybuilding in the true sense of the word. You are looking for exercises that will develop sufficient strength and power to improve your karate techniques. A whole body routine three times per week is sufficient. Avoid training the same muscle groups on consecutive days since this will lead to over-training.

To perform squats, rest the bar across your shoulders and keep your back straight, turning your feet slightly outwards and pushing your knees out, *fig. 105*. Then lower yourself carefully into the half squat position, *fig. 106*. To slightly change the emphasis of training, hold a lighter weight in front of your shoulders supported on your upper arms, *fig. 107*. This works the front of the thighs a little harder, *fig. 108*.

Using squats as the example, start off by doing 20 whilst just holding the bar. When you finish, add weights to the bar and do fifteen more. Put yet more weight on the bar and try for ten, then add more weight again and do five last squats. This method gives both an endurance and a power benefit and is called 'pyramid' training.

Beware the effects of momentum when doing squats using weights. Don't go beyond a half squat and don't bounce. Do let the weight come to rest before you drive it back up again.

108

THREE TO SIX MONTHS

For biceps curls, let the bar hang naturally in front of your thighs, gripping it about shoulder width, *fig. 109*. Keeping elbows in to your sides, quickly lift the bar up to your chin, *fig. 110*, and hold it there for a second, *fig. 111*, before lowering it back to the thighs. Don't drop the bar down quickly and don't involve the lower back in the exercise.

109

110

111

THREE TO SIX MONTHS

The shoulder, or 'military' press takes the bar from in front of the shoulders, *fig. 112*, to above the head in a smooth fast movement, *fig. 113*.

Note that the grip is wider than shoulder width. Lower the bar slowly back down to the shoulders. For maximum shoulder effect you don't need to lock the elbows.

112

113

Lift the bar over your head and rest it lightly across the back of the shoulders, *fig. 114*. Push it smartly up into a full press, *fig. 115*, hold for a second and then lower it back down across the back of the neck once more. This uses a slightly different training effect.

114

115

Lean forwards with the bar still on the back of the shoulders to perform the 'good morning' exercise, *fig. 116*, and hold for a few seconds before returning. This is a good exercise for the lower back.

116

117

Place the bar on the floor in front of you and grasp it overhand fashion using a grip wider than your slightly splayed feet, *fig. 117*. Using the muscles in your back, lift the bar with straight arms, *fig. 118*, and bring your trunk to an upright position, the bar hanging across the front of your thighs, *fig. 119*. Pull your shoulders back. This is the 'straight leg dead lift' exercise for the lower back muscles.

118

119

120

Set the bar on the floor and bend your knees slightly, *fig. 120*. Straighten your back and legs and pull the bar to shoulder height. As you step back, *fig. 121*, press the bar above your head, then step up to your original position to complete the exercise, *fig. 122*.

121

122

123

124

126

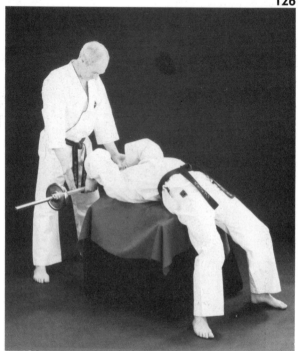

For safety's sake always use a partner when you train on the bench. Lie on your back and receive the bar, gripping it with a wide spaced hold, *fig. 123*, and gently lowering it to your chest, *fig. 124*.

Drive it up from your body in a fast smooth movement, *fig. 125*. To involve the triceps more use a narrow grip.

With your partner watching closely, lower the bar over and behind your head, *fig. 126*, then trying not to move your elbows, straighten your arms, *fig. 127*. This is known as the lying triceps extension.

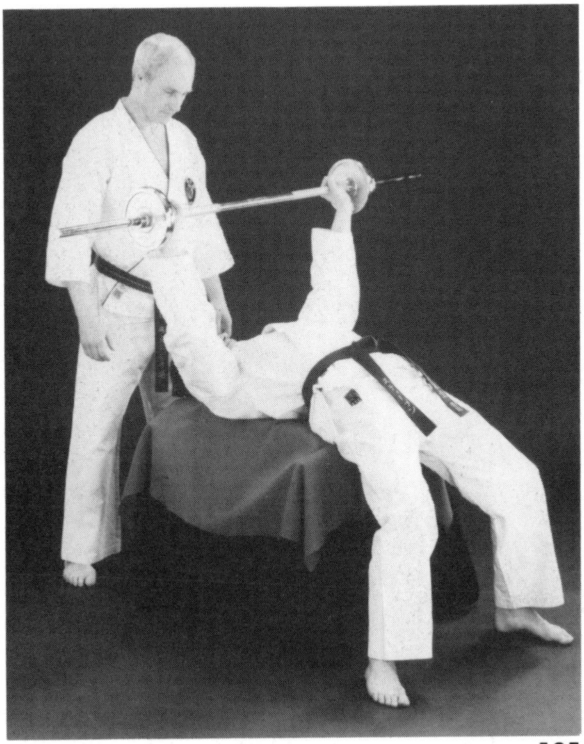

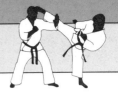

125

127

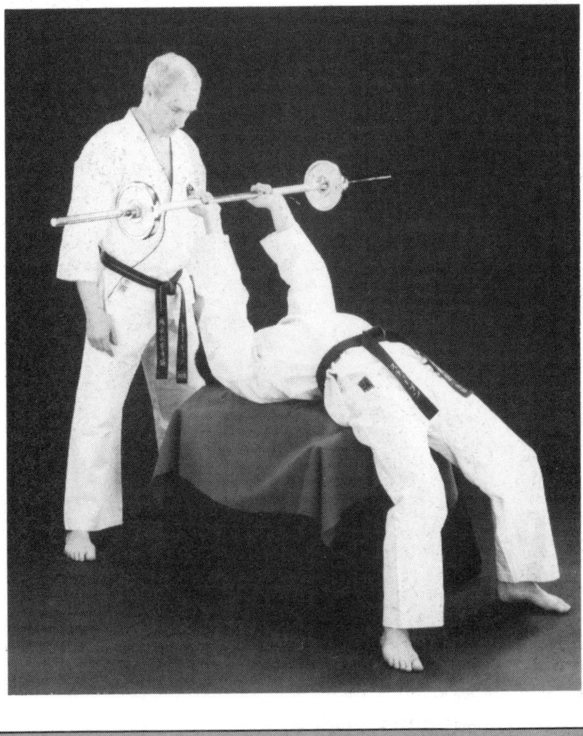

128

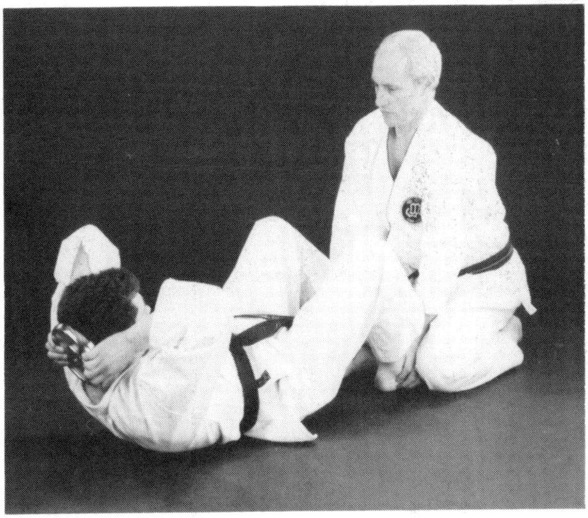

Follow on this series of exercises with weighted sit-ups. Keep your knees well bent whilst your partner holds your feet down to stop them rising. Clasp the weight behind your neck, or on your chest and sit up quickly, *fig. 128*.

In all the above cases, settle slowly into the exercise and then push strongly and quickly against the weight. It takes more energy to move a weight quickly than slowly. Do not use the momentum of the moving weight since this will lessen the training effect as can be seen in badly done biceps curls. The weight is dropped quickly down to the thighs and as it is about to come to rest, the thighs are pushed forwards, bumping it upwards.

129

Develop a grip of steel

Take a piece of broomhandle and drill a small hole through its diameter. Pass a piece of narrow nylon sash cord through the hole and knot it so it can't pull straight through. Wrap the other end around something heavy like a brick or sash weight and wind it up and down with a twisting action of your wrist.

If no weights are available to you, then either use what comes to hand, or go for heavier bodyweight exercises. As an example, you can load press-ups by putting your feet on a bench. To work your triceps harder, use the two chairs in the manner described earlier but this time rest your feet on a third chair, so more weight goes onto your arms. Drape your partner across your shoulders in a fireman's lift as you do squats. Lie on your back with your bottom pressed against the skirting board and your legs pointing straight up in the air to do abdominal crunches.

After weight training, switch over to flexibility work and concentrate on those areas that need attention. Remember that strength training shortens muscles and can lead to loss of flexibility, if stretching is neglected.

131

Use a partner to increase training effect by getting him/her to apply gradually increasing pressure whilst you try to keep the part being stretched completely relaxed. When the stretch becomes uncomfortable, signal your partner to apply no more pressure and hold position for a count of at least ten before relaxing.

Use a partner for assisted front-facing lift. Put your foot on your partner's shoulder and straighten your knee, *fig. 129*. Your partner should slowly force your leg higher until you signal for a stop. Keep your supporting foot flat on the floor and your hands to your sides as you hold the highest position for a count of ten. Then turn sideways-on to your partner and extend your foot. In exactly the same way your foot is gradually lifted higher and held at the position of maximum stretch, *fig. 130*.

Reach up and behind you, stretching both arms back as far as they will go. Your partner pulls on your straight arms, lifting them up and back whilst bracing you with a knee, *fig. 131*.

130

THREE TO SIX MONTHS

Train for agility by doing short sprints with sudden changes in direction of at least 90° with the minimum hesitation. Bound from side to side in a slalom run and switch fighting stance from left to right several times over in quick succession.

The impact pad is one of the finest training aids available for competition because it allows you to actually strike a target that has the same mass as your opponent. The best pads are sandwiches of closed cell resilient plastic foam sandwiching a softer foam central layer. The various layers are welded together so they can't come apart.

Be careful the first time you use an impact pad because many traditional karateka, even of black belt grade are so used to punching and kicking only against the empty air that they are completely at a loss when it comes to striking a pad. Unless you take care, you can sprain your wrist or over-stretch a joint.

Don't be surprised if you fall over the first time you kick the pad hard. Recoil from striking a man-mass can have surprising effects upon stability for a karateka brought up strictly in traditional karate training.

The pad is held either against the chest or the upper arm depending upon the technique to be used. The upper arm position is easier for receiving strong kicks, *fig. 132*, and it may even be necessary to lean into the pad to avoid the severe impact.

Go into the basic stance and make the techniques slowly at first, gradually building up speed as you get more confident. Your partner stands upright with feet apart and for all hand techniques he need not lean into the technique. The object is to develop a fast focused impact that explodes on the pad.

132

You should aim to punch in a relaxed manner, accelerating your technique into the target pad without fear of injury, *fig. 133*. If there is too much resistance to impact, you will not punch so quickly and training effect will be lost.

As you slide forward turn your hip slightly away and as range closes, swing it forwards with shoulders and arm following in a sort of whiplash effect. Don't move your hip and shoulder forward at the same time because you will lose the elasticity effect that catapults the fist out from your side and into the target.

133

THREE TO SIX MONTHS

The pad must be angled slightly downwards for front kick, otherwise the foot can slip up and into the face, *fig. 134*. Stand sideways on to the opponent for roundhouse kick, with the leading leg on the same side as the leading edge of the pad, *fig. 135*.

Don't tilt the pad so the toes land first or you will hyperextend the toe joints. Impact is with the instep. Hold the pad in the same way for training reverse roundhouse kick, *fig. 136*.

For competition training always strike the pad with controlled force and do not attempt full power impacts with any technique because these are not used in WUKO competition.

135

134

136

I use the pad for training footsweeps by getting the partner to sit down and partly extend one leg. The pad is held against the leg, *fig. 137*, whilst you swing your foot around and into it. Keep your foot just above the floor and catch the pad with the sole of your foot, *fig. 138*. Hit the pad with sufficient force to spin your partner around. Lean away from the impact because if you are successful in a real sweep, the opponent may lash out as he goes down.

137

139

Moving onto skill acquisition, I want now to describe the usage of foot sweeps and hooks. First of all it is easier to sweep an opponent who is moving than one standing still. If the opponent is about to put weight on his foot as you sweep it, the technique will be far more effective but if the opponent is settled in a strong stance, the footsweep is not a technique of choice. Use a footsweep against an opponent in a weak stance.

Four basic sweeping techniques are most used in competition karate. The ankle can be attacked from the outside at a 90° angle to where the foot is pointing. This is generally used when the opponent's foot is moving to the side anyway, *figs 139 & 140*.

140

The front of the shin or ankle can also be attacked when the opponent leans forward over the front knee, *fig. 141*. A solid hit with the sole of your foot applied then will drop the opponent flat on his face in front of you.

When the opponent has put his knee behind his heel so the centre of gravity is closer to the rear foot, the front foot can be swept from behind, drawing it out in the direction it is pointing, *fig. 142*.

141

142

Be careful with this last sweeping technique because you need to get close to the opponent during delivery – so a good guard is essential.

The inside of the ankle can also be swept so the opponent's stance is widened and he lurches forwards off balance, *fig. 143.*

Always be careful to attack only the lower part of the opponent's leg when using a foot sweep. You can earn an immediate penalty for one that appears to the referee to be a direct attack on a limb or joint.

Hooking techniques use a pull rather than a jarring impact. You hook your foot behind your opponent's ankle as he is settling weight on to the front leg, then draw it up and towards you. The basic hook normally uses the front foot rather than the rear foot favoured by sweeping techniques.

143

144

Whilst correct form requires you to hook the opponent's foot with the sole of your foot, in practice you will tend to use the inside edge.

A very practical hooking technique is to use a roundhouse kick-like sweep to the opponent's leading ankle. First position yourself so your front foot is in line with your opponent's. Then act as though you were going to use a roundhouse kick but aim your knee down at the opponent's leading ankle and slap into the back of it with a diving roundhouse kick.

Your foot curls around the back of the opponent's ankle, *fig. 144*, and drags the foot forwards, *fig. 145*.

Turn fully on your supporting leg and lean well away from the possibility of counter attack. If the opponent lifts his front leg so your attack skates on past, let it go in the direction it is moving and pivot on your supporting leg to turn back to face him.

Used in this way the hook is marginally safer than the foot sweep because if the latter misses, you tend to fall directly into the opponent's counter-attack. The possibility of knee injury is also lessened because the attacking foot is pointing in the same direction as the foot being attacked.

145

146

Begin pair-form sparring by having your opponent attack you with front kick, *fig. 146*. Deflect the kick to one side, using a scooping block, *fig. 147*. As the opponent is about to touch down, spin around, *fig. 148*, and hit his leg with the back of your ankle, *fig. 149*, before full weight has descended onto it. This will topple him onto his back in front of you, *fig. 150*, and you can follow with a punch to score a full point, *fig. 151*.

There is an obvious danger in that you are turning your back on the opponent and all he has to do is lift his front foot over the sweep and strike you full in the back for a one point score. On the other hand it is an unexpected move and this may give you a tactical advantage. Don't try it if your deflection block has been less than successful!

147

148

149

150

151

152

For the yet more agile performer, drop under an incoming roundhouse kick to the head and turn into it, *fig. 152*. Keep your body low and scythe the back of your calf into his supporting leg. If you catch him whilst his foot is still high in the air he will land hard on his backside.

I want now to talk about combination techniques. These are two or more potentially scoring techniques linked together so one quickly follows the other. Typically, successive techniques will be aimed at different targets so the opponent's attention is diverted from where it is you want to attack properly.

The speed of the combination sequence is very important because the opponent must not perceive the individual techniques which make it up in time to recognise the cues and respond effectively. In a two technique sequence, the follow-up attack must be so fast that the opponent doesn't have time to retrieve the first response. Never wait for the opponent to actually counter your first technique before launching the second.

Distinguish between combination techniques and a feint/follow-up sequences on the grounds that a feint isn't intended to score. It is a sudden movement designed to confuse the opponent whilst the scoring technique proper is used. By comparison, each separate element of a combination technique is capable of scoring in its own right.

Feint/attack sequences tend to be used more frequently than combination attacks in today's competition.

From the scoring point of view it is not a good idea to use more than three techniques in any combination because both technique, quality and power fall off rapidly when techniques are used in rapid succession. Moreover with a melee of arms and legs flying about it becomes very difficult for the referee to distinguish what is and what is not a scoring technique.

Perhaps the most basic combination is to attack the face with a leading hand snap punch, *fig. 153*, and then drop down and deliver a follow-up reverse punch to the opponent's ribs, *fig. 154*. This works because the opening punch directs the opponent's attention upwards, creating a window through which the score can be made.

153

154

THREE TO SIX MONTHS

Another common combination uses perhaps a right reverse punch to the body, *fig. 155*, and even as it is being withdrawn, a right roundhouse kick to the head follows it, *fig. 156*. A form of converse, though this is really a feint/attack, works well for those with less flexible hips. Reverse punch to the opponent's face and as he responds with a high block, use a mid-section roundhouse kick to his ribs, *fig. 157*.

155

156

157

Face your partner with both of you in a left stance. Close to fighting range and suddenly reach forwards with your rear hand, slapping his forward guard hand to the side, *fig. 158.*

158

As you deflect it, step quickly forward with the rear leg, placing it to the outside of your opponent's and punch, *fig. 159*, with the other hand.

159

TACTICS REVISITED

Before a competition I like to see how my next opponent fights so I watch him in action on the area, noting his favourite techniques and looking for a pattern of behaviour that I can recognise. If I haven't seen him fighting before, I look at him and study his physique. Are there any signs of nervousness?

Once in the area I move around, looking at how he moves. Is there any weakness in his stance? Does he lapse into a common pattern of movement every now and again?

I make sudden fast moves towards him and break off before they turn into attacks. How does he react? Does he back off smartly or does he stand his ground? How quickly does he react to feints?

If he attacks strongly I go into him and meet his attack because I happen to prefer a counter-attacking role. I will try to draw him onto the offensive by offering openings to try for. As he moves forward I will skip back quickly, even if his advance is only half-hearted. I keep opening up the distance between us so that if he wants to attack, he's got to make a forward step first. This will encourage him to think that I'm not going to stand my ground and the next time he comes in, he over-extends and that is when I counter-attack.

Respond as soon as your opponent makes a forward step. Don't wait for the attack itself and that way you won't have to worry whether it is a kick or punch. A skilled attacker may launch the attack without giving you a clear cue. If this happens be prepared to block and counter, or step back from him. It is always riskier to try and interpret an attack once it has begun.

Blocks are in themselves of limited use. They stop the attack from reaching you but they must always be followed with a scoring technique, *fig. 160*. You can't keep just blocking every technique because sooner or later one will get through.

TACTICS REVISITED

Always stop the opponent at the earliest possible time because once he begins using combination attacks, things start getting very difficult to handle.

Some people tell you to watch the opponent's eyes as a method of telling when an attack is imminent. I personally look at the mouth because just before a committed attack the opponent takes a sharp breath in and often tightens his facial muscles. The more anxious or faster the attack, the more the face gives away the intent.

Therefore if you want to draw your attacker more effectively, suck air in noisily and contort your face as you make a large jerky movement. This will be more readily responded to than a smooth short movement.

Break your timing. Begin advancing strongly and then suddenly pause, *fig. 161*. To range an incoming target effectively, your opponent must throw his technique early so it is travelling at maximum speed when the target actually comes into range. Instants after launching it, the opponent realises you have stopped and he will immediately try to draw back his attack. It is during this time that you resume your attack and score, *fig. 162*.

161

Do not miss the contrast here. If you want a successful feint, make a large movement that can't be mistaken. If you want a successful attack, make your movement as smooth as possible and try to disguise your intention until the last possible instant.

Even quite slow smooth attacks sometimes succeed because they don't look threatening.

Do remember to make your feint inside the opponent's reaction range. This is the distance where the opponent will feel threatened by a sudden move and react. A feint outside this distance no matter how spectacular, will not achieve the same degree of diversion.

Remember that your opponent will be watching you too in order to discern any kind of a pattern. Don't fall into a common sequence of moves and do try to attack spontaneously when you might be least expected to. Don't even think consciously of attacking, because in some way a premeditated attack can be read even before it begins. If your attacker is working himself up to attack you, then that is the time to take the attack to him – when he is least expecting it.

162

TACTICS REVISITED

If you tell your opponent that you are going to attack with roundhouse kick to the head, he will have little trouble in countering it, no matter how fast you put it in. If you tell him you are going to do a front kick, *fig. 163*, but then suddenly change it to a roundhouse kick in the last instant, chances are you will score, *fig. 164*. You will increase the chances of success further if you pretend to attack a couple of times beforehand with a normal front kick, so your opponent believes he starts to recognise a pattern.

163

164

Telegraphing a technique tells the opponent what is about to come at him and so a skilled contestant will deliberately choose confusing cues.

A telegraphed front kick is easily recognised and even as the front knee begins to rise, the opponent is driving in off the back leg and reverse punching to the chest. A bent arm guard held forward is enough to fend off the rising knee because it has not yet developed a great deal of power. The other hand drives in a reverse punch for a possible full point score, *fig. 165.*

165

On the other hand, that telegraphed front kick could just as easily be a feint. As the knee rises into the attacker's reaction area, the latter dives forward and attempts to deflect/stop punch it, *fig. 166*, only to find that you have halted the kick half way. You then jump forwards to the outside of the opponent's front leg and waste no time in throwing a strong but controlled face punch, *fig. 167*.

When the opponent's foot rises to the side of the body, you can immediately read the unmistakable cue for an incipient roundhouse kick and counter it, *fig. 168*.

166

167

168

TACTICS REVISITED

169

Distance is quite important and many people let the opponent get too close, so he can hit you without stepping forward. This is bad practice because unless you are extremely good at defence techniques and have lightning fast reactions, his technique will reach you before you have the chance to respond effectively.

Kicks take much longer to recover. The leg has to be brought back, both feet placed on the ground and both balance and guard re-established. So always be ready to counter-attack quickly when a kick has missed.

Many fighters throw kicks without any regard for their target. This is why so many fail to score.

Others make the mistake of throwing a roundhouse kick for example when they are badly positioned. The distance may be fine but the kick is easily blocked, *fig. 169*. Why is that? The answer could lie in the line you have taken.

170

Imagine that your opponent faces you in left stance and you are in the same stance. Your leading foot is more or less in line with their rear foot as you turn your hips into the kick. If you examine this scenario carefully, you will see that as your body rotates, it is brought into easy range of the opponent's reverse punch. The situation is even more hazardous if you keep your body upright or hinged forward.

If on the other hand your left foot is in line with your opponent's left foot, then not only will the range of your roundhouse kick be increased by as much as 18 inches but with your body leaning back it will be almost impossible to reach you with that same reverse punch, *fig. 170*.

Don't use a roundhouse kick if your opponent is circling in the direction your kick will travel because he is moving away from it and can block it easily, *fig. 171*. Swap legs quickly and aim against the direction of rotation so he moves into it, *fig. 172*. If you use a strong feint attack first he may not see the roundhouse until it hits him. Even if he does see it, his circling movement does not equip him for making an effective block.

When you and your opponent are both in left stance, a left roundhouse kick will stand a better chance of success because there are more targets for it to go for. The right foot has to clear shoulder and elbow to reach the head, *fig. 173*, and even a mid-section attack is out unless the opponent is holding his forward guard hand too high.

171

172

173

Maintain the aerobic training programme though by now you will be able to train near the top of the aerobic training band. By now also you should have developed your local muscular endurance to support the level of technique delivery that you expect.

The flexibility programme continues with more advanced training utilising what is called the 'PNF' method. At this stage I would expect you to be much more supple and better able to benefit from this form of training. As I have said before, do not attempt stretching until you have been through a good warm-up session.

To illustrate the principles of PNF stretching I have chosen an exercise we are already familiar with. Sit down and gather your legs in close, soles of feet together. Take hold of your ankles and press downwards on your knees with your elbows. If you are working with a partner, get them to apply firm pressure down onto the knees so the muscles on the insides of the thighs – the 'thigh adductors' – are stretched. Relax and hold the lowest position for a count of ten seconds and then ease up for two to four seconds before pressure is applied again.

This time, when you reach the low position, contract your thigh adductors, resisting the pushing force. Hold this contraction for about ten seconds and then relax once more.

Apply firm pressure once more to push the knees gently downwards but now it will be found that they go down further. Hold them in this new lowest position for a count of 30 seconds before releasing. Repeat the stretch two or three times.

Remember not to stretch until pain is felt because this is counterproductive. You should experience no more than mild discomfort if your flexibility programme is to proceed efficiently.

This enhanced exercise is particularly useful for improving hip flexibility in relation to the roundhouse, reverse roundhouse and side kick.

To stretch the muscles in the backs of the thighs, sit down with your legs outstretched in front of you. Reach forward and take hold of your feet, pulling down until you are in the lowest position with your head up and looking forwards. Keep your back straight and try not to curve your spine too much.

Hold this position for ten seconds and then relax before trying to force yourself back up by tightening your hamstrings against the grip on your feet. Relax once more and sink back down again to the new lowest position, holding that for 30 seconds.

Alternatively lie on your back and lift a straight leg up into the air. Your partner takes hold of your foot and pulls it back towards your shoulders. When it is stretched as far as possible, relax for a few seconds, then try to force your leg back down again whilst your partner resists you. After ten seconds of this, relax and allow the leg to be stretched again.

Women karateka suffer more than men from short achilles tendons. A good remedial exercise is to lean against a wall in a long forward stance and push the heel back down to the floor. Hold it there for ten seconds and then press down with the ball of the foot, raising the heel. Maintain this for ten seconds and then relax. Finally resume the heel down position and this time you will find it easier to press flat to the floor. Hold this final position as before.

Alternatively stand on a step and let your heel drop below the level. Thrust down on the ball of the foot and raise the heel; then lower it back down again.

Plyometrics is a new area of training which paradoxically has been long recognised by practitioners of my own style of karate – *shukokai*. The principle of plyometrics is that a stretched muscle is loaded with potential energy.

174

175

176

Try it by crouching down into a half squat and when in position jump as high as you can. Measure your height. Then bob down from a standing position into the half squat immediately before driving upwards. This time you will jump higher because you prestretched the muscles in the front of your thighs and by doing that, loaded them with energy.

As you throw your reverse punch try to 'separate' the movement of the hip and shoulder, *fig. 174*. In other words drive the hip forward, stretching the chest and arching your back. This loads the pectoral muscle and whips the arm forward at a much greater rate of acceleration, *figs 175-176*.

SIX TO NINE MONTHS

In the same way, as you kick, your hips drive forward and the stomach muscles are stretched. The lower leg lags behind the rapidly rising upper and the muscles on the front of the thighs are also stretched. When the lower leg is driven out, these pre-stretched muscles contract with greater power and the kick is faster.

During the roundhouse kick, the upper body rotates and leans away, the back arches, producing stretching of the muscles of the abdomen and hip. This lends additional power to the kick as it follows along behind.

By now you will be able to hit the impact pad quickly and effectively with a variety of techniques and it is the correct time for learning how to zero in on a moving pad. Get your partner to hold the pad against the chest and then move suddenly into or away from you. You have a split second in which to respond to either hitting the pad as it comes towards you, or taking a quick slide-back step if you've left it late and distance has closed below the optimal for focus.

If the pad moves away, chase after it quickly and close distance sufficiently to be able to hit it with a controlled degree of force.

Start this type of training slowly, or you may sprain your wrist.

Use a target mitt to improve accuracy and if one isn't available, tie a belt around an impact pad and get your partner to hold it from behind. He/she stands fairly close to you and holds the pad down against the thigh, *fig. 177*. Suddenly it is swung up to present the face or side to you and you have to respond quickly, choosing the correct technique to hit it accurately and with focus.

If the pad is presented directly towards you at head height, attack it with snap punch, *fig. 178*. If it is turned sideways-on, use either back fist, *fig. 179*, roundhouse kick, or reverse roundhouse kick, *fig. 180*.

As you get better at it, have your partner move around, closing and pulling quickly back so you have to deal with a moving target presented at different heights. Your partner must not whip the pad quickly out of the way of your incoming attack since that can overload your joints. Once presented, the pad is left out until your technique connects with it.

This fast form of training requires good coordination and agility. It is also very useful for teaching focus and control, both of which are important if a technique is to score.

178

177

179

180

SIX TO NINE MONTHS

Rely heavily on kata training during this late stage of your preparation. Do several full speed repetitions in succession as a means of building in combination sequences whilst simultaneously undergoing whole body endurance training. Make the techniques explosive but don't lock your arms and legs out against the empty air. Concentrate on the shorin-based katas because their quick movements promote agility and coordination.

Maintain a high standard of technique throughout the kata because it is all too easy to start throwing poor quality punches and kicks which would never score in a competition. Remember, it is very difficult to unlearn bad habits. Use a mirror to check your performance.

The kata I have selected for your study is 'Rohei'. This is an Okinawan kata comprising equal measures of agility, speed and power. It is a fairly short kata, as katas go and one which is not seen often. It is relatively easy to learn and encapsulates all the benefits which accrue to kata practice.

SIX TO NINE MONTHS

Go for higher order combination techniques in your prearranged sparring and make use of all the information given in the last chapter on ways of mis-cueing the opponent. Throw a roundhouse kick at your opponent's head, *fig. 181*, and as he attempts to block, bring it straight down into a hook behind the ankle, *figs 182 & 183*. Look out for the opponent's arms flailing about as he falls off balance and step in quickly to punch for a full point score, *fig. 184*.

181

182

183

184

185

186

Practise high speed punch switching combinations allied to changes in line. For example, begin from left stance with a strong reverse punch to the opponent's head, *fig. 185*. To achieve the necessary diversion, first close to an effective distance.

Even as this first punch is completing, begin stepping diagonally out to the side of the opponent's front foot, *fig. 186*, and slam in a mid-section reverse punch as you drop weight onto the front foot, *fig. 187*. Strike high in the body, where it is more difficult to block.

Start with a similar attack but this time reverse punch to the opponent's chest. As you begin pulling the punch back, snap punch to the face with your left hand, closing range by sliding the front foot forwards. Aim slightly to the side of the opponent's face so he fails to see the mid-section reverse punch that begins even as the snap punch is being withdrawn.

187

188

189

Attack with front kick from left fighting stance and just as it attracts a block, *fig. 188*, switch it into a roundhouse kick to the head, *fig. 189*. In this case the opponent has seen the sudden change and starts to lift his guard hand to ward off the kick. A quick counter-attack is not possible because your line is correct and you are leaning away.

As you pull the foot back, *fig. 190*, suddenly launch yourself forwards with the right foot and deliver a low ranging reverse punch. Choose your landing point so you drop down to the outside of your opponent's leading foot, *fig. 191*.

190

191

Keep training until the week before your competition but in these final stages, ease up on the heavy endurance work in favour of lighter training allied to more complicated skill acquisition. The day before the big event you should rest and try to relax.

Do some gentle stretching exercises but avoid anything that taxes your strength. The object is to arrive on the day feeling fit and full of beans, not burnt out and shattered through excessive training.

Good luck!

AUTHOR'S NOTE

I would like gratefully to acknowledge the help I have received in writing this book from my son Steven. He willingly acted as my partner in the photographs and helped to portray effectively the techniques I wanted to show.

I also gratefully acknowledge the assistance of Jennie Sanders, an ex-British international who is now devoting her considerable expertise to the teaching of tomorrow's world champions.

Thanks too to David Mitchell for his assistance in the preparation and editing of this text. David is a karateka himself and his considerable knowledge of other styles prompted me to consider areas of training that I might otherwise have missed.

Finally a big thank you to all the students of Kobe Osaka Karate Clubs for their hard training and numerous successes in major competitions. Their progress and improvement has been my motivation to continue.

Tommy Morris,
Glasgow 1987.

Further Information: Those wishing to learn more of Tommy Morris' karate techniques should write to him at Kobe-Osaka Ltd., 68 Glassford St, Glasgow G1 1UP.

Steven Morris – European silver medallist kata, Glasgow, 1987.

GLOSSARY

These are some of the terms used in karate competition. They are not accurate translations of the Japanese but this is what they mean in practical terms:

Shobuippon hajime : "Three point contest – begin!"

Yamei : "Stop"

Tsuzukete hajime : "Re-start the contest"

Shobu hajime : "Extension – begin!"

Moto-no-ichi : "Return to your standing line"

Ippon : "One point"

Waza-ari : "Half point"

Keikoku : "Half point penalty"

Hansoku-chui : "One point penalty"

Hansoku : "Foul"

Shikkaku : "Disqualification"

Jogai : "Outside area"

Mubobi : "Failing to ensure own safety"

Aka : "Red"

Shiro : "White"

Hantei : "Decision"

Kiken : "Withdrawal"

Aka – kiken : "Red withdraws"

Aka no-kachi : "Red wins"

Aka ippon : "Red gains one point"

Aka keikoku : "Red is penalised by half point"

Shiro waza-ari : "White gains half point"

Kata : A form of training using whole series of combination techniques. Katas may be short or long and stress a particular number of aspects of karate practice, such as stance, agility, speed and stamina.

Learn the terminology to understand the rules.

GLOSSARY OF FORBIDDEN DRUGS

The following drugs must not be taken by any person competing in karate competition:

Psychomotor Stimulants

Amphetamine
Benzphetamine
Chlorphentermine
Cocaine
Diethylpropion
Dimethylamphetamine
Ethylamphetamine
Fencamfamin
Meclofenoxate
Methylamphetamine
Methylphenidate
Norpseudoephedrine
Pemoline
Phendimetrazine
Phenmetrazine
Phentermine
Pipradol
Prolintane

Sympathomimetic Amines

Clorprenaline
Ephedrine
Etafedrine
Isoetharine
Isoprenaline
Methylephedrine
Methoxyphenamine

Miscellaneous CNS Stimulants

Amiphenazole
Bemegride
Doxapram
Ethamivan
Leptazol
Nikethamide
Picrotoxin
Strychnine

Narcotic Analgesics

Anileridine
Codeine
Dextromoramide
Dihydrocodeine
Dipipanone
Ethylmorphine
Heroin
Hydrocodone
Hydromorphone
Levorphanol
Methadone
Morphine
Oxocodone
Oxomorphone
Pentazocine
Pethidine
Phenazocine
Piminodine
Thebacon
Trimeperidine

Anabolic Steroids

Clostebol
Ethyloestranol
Fluoxymesterone
Methandienone
Methenolone
Methandriol
Methyltestosterone
Nandralone
Oxandrolone
Oxymetholone
Stanolone
Stanozolol

And other related compounds in all categories.

INDEX